PADDLE HOME

poems + passages

AMBER LILYESTROM

*You are an ocean of possibility,
limitless and immeasurable, reaching depths
only the heart can ever know.*

Copyright 2021 © Amber Lilyestrom

First published in 2021
by KMD Books
Waikiki, WA 6169

All rights reserved. No part of this book may be used or reproduced by any means, graphic, electronic, or mechanical, including photocopying, recording, taping or by any information storage retrieval system without the written permission of the copyright owner except in the case of brief quotations embodied in critical articles and reviews. Although the author and publisher have made every effort to ensure that the information in this book was correct at press time, the author and publisher do not assume and hereby disclaim any liability to any party for any loss, damage, or disruption caused by errors or omissions, whether such errors or omissions result from negligence, accident, or any other cause. This book is not intended as a substitute for the medical advice of physicians. The reader should regularly consult a physician in matters relating to his/her health and particularly with respect to any symptoms that may require diagnosis or medical attention.

Interior and cover design: Cassandra Neece
Photographs: Lauren Bodwell and Daniel Aaron Sprague (pages 49 and 122)

National Library of Australia Catalogue-in-Publication data:
Paddle Home/Amber Lilyestrom

ISBN: 978-0-6451353-1-2 (sc)
ISBN: 978-0-6451353-2-9 (e)

PADDLE HOME

poems + passages

AMBER LILYESTROM

To my darling Annika, no matter where the stream takes you, may you always find your way back home to the truth of who you are, to the beat of your precious heart, to the remembrance of the miracle that is you.

I love you, always + forever.

FOREWORD
by Adrea Peters

I have the incomprehensible pleasure of sitting across from many new writers.

They are scared. Sometimes too terrified to utter a word.

I push all their buttons before I have spoken. No matter what I do, or say, or cross out, or question, they are shattered. It brings me unadulterated joy because it's how I know they are a writer. A real writer. The kind that cares deeply about the reader. The kind that knows the power of the written, and spoken, word. The kind that becomes more only when they lock themselves to the pages of their stories.

I know they are in my good hands. I am them. This means I know, ready or not, their writing is everything to them. Hurting them, hurts me. I do it anyway because that's how we get better. We have to go there and feel it all. We can't help it and nor should we.

Doubt is all consuming to us writers. Over time we learn to live with it, perhaps outsmart and hoodwink it, yet it lingers. It's the non-mystical force behind our endless procrastination.

And then.

From time to time.

A writer swallows doubt whole and lets it participate on the page. Asking it to come over, sit and stay awhile, have tea, become friends. This is when the writer becomes an author.

Years ago, five to be exact, Amber swallowed her doubt, and journeyed thousands of miles from her home for the first time, to join me and an extraordinary cadre of writers for a writing retreat in Hawaii. This sweet soul arrived terrified and left, slightly less terrified, and absolutely committed to her writing.

It gives me profound honor to witness her shed her writer and step into her author.

Paddle Home goes beyond what I imagined it might. I've read many iterations and gleefully watched more and more of Amber arrive to the page creating an exquisite memoir told in delicate spoonfuls of insight and reassurance.

She holds you as you read. Do you understand the magnitude of such an offering?

You will.

May you exhale as you imagine her waiting by the shore as you paddle your way home, dear soul. This is where you begin.

Congratulations, my dear, Amber. I'm insanely proud of you.

All love, always.

adrea.

All of you is welcome here. You belong. All of you is welcome here. You

Welcome Home

We have a sign that hangs in the entryway of our home that reads "All of you is welcome here."

I had this piece created as a daily reminder and invitation as we cross over the threshold of our sacred space.

I share these words at the start of our journey together here to invite you into the safe space that I hope this book will be for you.

Paddle Home has been writing me for the last decade of my life. I have traveled thousands of miles with these passages hidden in notebooks, only partially conceived inside my mind until it was time to trust the words that welcomed me home each day I walked through the door.

"All of you is welcome here."

So I pass along this sweet baton to you...

Every half-baked dream, cloaked musing, sacred story and gorgeous worry that waits within you is welcome here. Your secrets, your craziest ideas, your desperate longings and your deepest heartache are all part of the wild wonder that is you.

I am so overjoyed for you witness what reveals itself along the stream.

With all my love + appreciation,

Amber

Paddle Home

It was a long day of mothering and making do.
I grabbed my boat and paddled out to the middle of the pond to commune with my spirit and the unseen.
The warming sun and brisk April winds enveloped me as I floated over the soft ripples.
My family played on the shore and the sound of their laughter lilted over the waves, reminding me of their ever-presence.

I breathed deeply, sinking into my plastic seat, letting what I could melt away.
I turned my thoughts over in my mind – ideas converging and skittering away as I exhaled myself into to the moment over and over again.
The words, "Paddle home" floated up from the depths.

Paddle Home.

Entranced by this sacred instruction, I turned my boat toward our shore and gently guided myself back – the way we do only when our seeking meets surrender.

And there it was - everything I've ever wanted.
Right before my very eyes, even in the moments I couldn't see it.
We are born holding the seeds of our own destiny.
Our holy work is to till the fertile soil of truth and tend to the seeds of our calling long before they bear fruit.
It is in the soft confessions and tumultuous reckonings that we remember to remember our dreams will require us to rise and reclaim the parts of us we lost along the way.
It turns out, the act of surrender, in and of itself, is the gateway to the grand prize we've been seeking.

As I neared the shore, my daughter ran to the end of the dock with her tiny arms outstretched and yelled, "You're home!"

"You're home!"

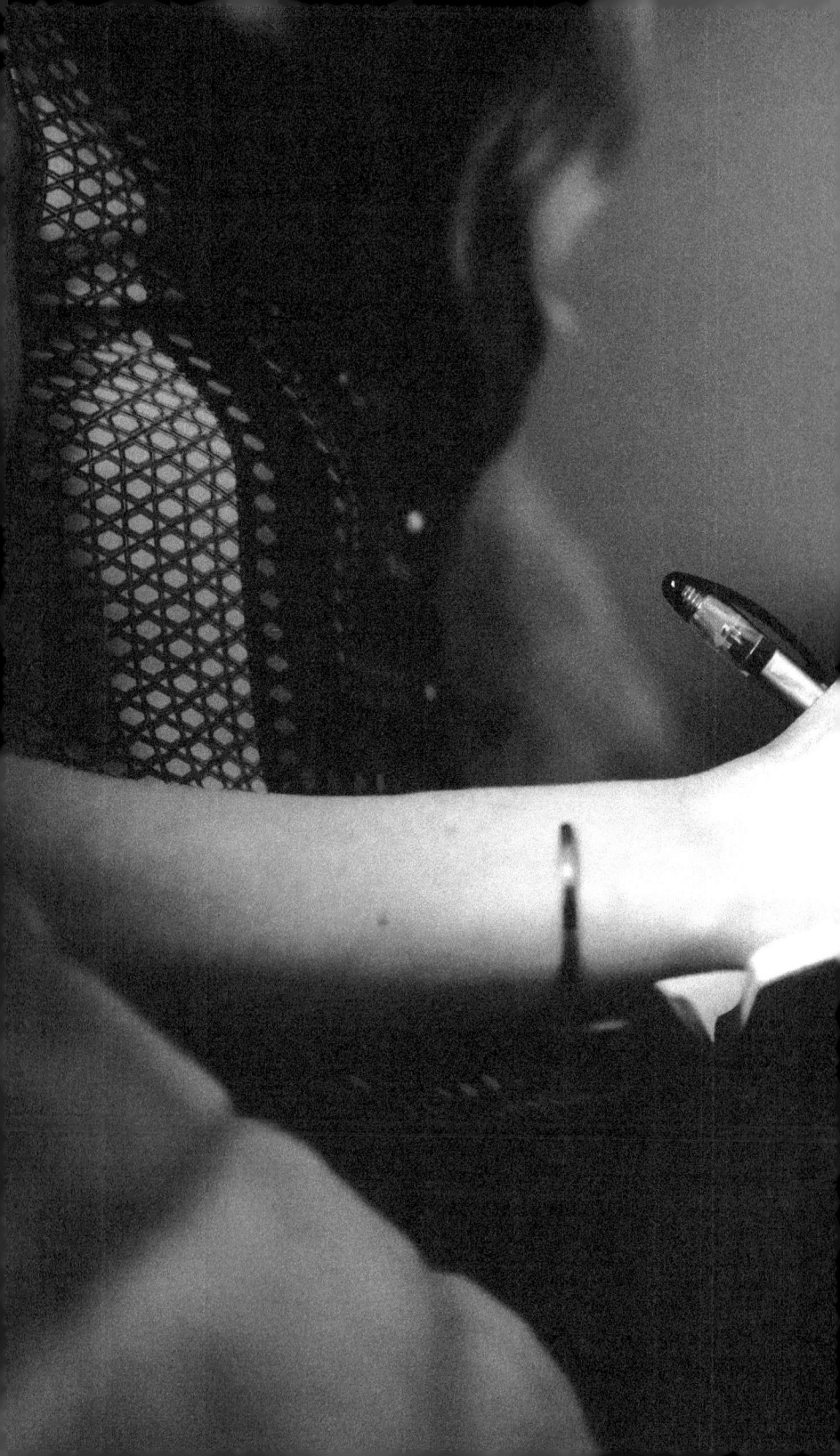

The Crossing

Cross over the threshold of your deepest truth.
Rest in the comfort of your unending spirit.
Transcend your titles.
Let go of your labels.
Tear down the walls of limitation and
inhabit all of who you are.
Live from this knowing.

Sea spray and skin

I saw a girl playing in the ocean wearing only sea spray and skin.
She was the type of free I have always longed to be.
Tangled in joy, she splashed in the waves and I wondered...
Who gave her permission to claim her beauty?

Everything is Sacred

Every single thing is sacred.
Every single moment carries in it the devotion of
the one before.
Life has a way of landing us in the rubble of what we've missed,
So we can still ourselves to see the stars.

Everything is sacred.
Everything is sacred.
Everything is sacred.
Even you.

Wings

I used to carry the weight of the world on my shoulders,
until I got too tired.
I handed over your possibility and your pain.
I returned your joy and your judgements.
I gave it all back and kept only what was mine.
We steadied ourselves in the space between.
Unclipped our wings.
And set ourselves free to fly.

The Most Courageous Thing

Someone I love very much got in the car and drove to my house so we could mend the broken fence between us.

Over roasted vegetables and copious glasses of water, we unearthed the hardest parts of our pain and cried tears of anguish and the deep sadness we'd carried with us for way too long.

We put down our swords and the stories we inherited from those who knew not what they did and cleared the slate with the only place we knew to go – home to love.
Over time, I've come to understand and adopt the notion that being in relationship with those I love is more important than being right.

This is not to say that I openly endure mistreatment, rather, I've learned to be the first one to put down my sword because my life is no longer about winning a battle where there is nothing to be won.

After almost dying and becoming a mother in the same day, holding grudges and harshly judging others no longer seemed like a useful practice or way to spend these precious days.

Thinking back to the most painful experiences of my lifetime,
there was always an experience of love being withheld,
whether consciously or unconsciously.
Because of this, I vowed that love would be my answer.
Underneath the weight of our trauma and the chaos that comes
with trying to right-side what simply cannot be,
we're all just big kids working to earn the love we craved.

And like the baton that is as old as time, we hand it down to our
children, knowing not what we do – other than the best we can.

Mending the fences of intergenerational trauma while paying
the taxes and driving the kids to soccer practice is trying work.

Unearthing our personal shame and what we've never been able
to understand, while healing our gut and going for that next
promotion is no joke.

So much is asked of us in the complex condition of being
here in these bodies.
Some days it's too much to bear.

But here we are, me – sitting crossed-legged atop the kitchen island and you- perched on the stool a few feet away with our shovels out and our head lamps on.

Together, we're digging up the parts of a past that never belonged to us along with those that do, our hearts wide open and voices breaking into tears around every turn.
And then we exhale and wash our tired hands of the dirt only to realize there was nothing to dig for after all.

The treasure is right here in this kitchen.

The Tidal Wave of Your Temper

You can be unhappy, and I can be ok.
The tidal wave of your temper has crashed through my heart
and home more times than I can recount.
I've rebuilt and dusted off my tender soul, time and time again.
I've come to know the way the wind feels, and the
seas swell when life crashes on your shore.
I've learned that the silence of the birds and the absence of
the fishermen out in the harbor can only mean one thing.
So, I batten down my hatches and close up all my doors.
I tell myself this time will be different and by degrees, I am
always right.
Your waves can no longer destroy me, only stir what's
still undone.
Here I sit in the silence and watch the scared creature that
inhabits my heart slow itself long enough to remain.
After a while, I fall asleep and dream of awakening to the
golden sunrise of a new day.

You are a different person in the mind of everyone you meet.

Be you for you.

Worth the Wait

Somewhere along the way we got the message that some part of us was mercilessly flawed.
Whether it was the body we walk through life with or a heart that feels too much, we learned that in order to fit, in order to matter, revisions were required.

For me, this was about my anger as a child.
I was angry about having to go to therapy to clean up the pieces of things I had not broken.
I was angry about having to say words little girls aren't supposed to say.
I was angry because I felt like a butterfly in a net on a warm summer's day.

So, I did what I could to make myself smaller, more accomplished and less of a burden.
I went about the business of living and striving to escape the weight of it all.
Each day another shovel full of earth removed, digging me deeper into the pit of my own self-loathing.
I was in the hole and nobody knew it.

I put on a happy face and made the honor roll.
I scored the goals and made the headlines.
I walked home from school alone and hid the evidence of
the sugar I used to soothe myself into sweetness.

If I could go back and look that beautiful girl in the eyes,
I would tell her to write and rage all over the page.
I would tell her that their pain was never hers to own.
I would tell her to dream beyond the bounds of her tidy
plans that included everyone's needs but her own.
I would tell her that her feelings were real and that they
matter even if no one had the space to hold them.
I would tell her that it will take what feels like a lifetime to
be truly known, but it will be worth the wait.

The Star

I was once the star player.
Until the rules of the game began to ask too much of me.
The roles I had to play.
The masks I had to wear.
The ways you loved the idea of me more than the truth of me.
I knew it was time to go.

Illuminate

Empty your pockets.
Empty your drawers.
Dump out all of your stories and your sorrow.
Strike a match and let the score cards burn.

Who are we without the weight of the world that we
have carried?
Who do we get to be when we drop the darkness
of our doubts?
We came from the light.
We will return to the light.
We are light in living motion.

Illuminate.

Growing Old

I sat on the back deck with Dad as we waited for Ben to return home from picking up pizza.

Dad just finished paddling around the pond and we were talking about his shaking hands.
He pointed out that it was just his left and only when he held it down by his side.
I pointed out that we didn't know enough yet
to know anything.
Both of us sat in the quiet clinging to our hope in a
sea of uncertainty.

We talked about his upcoming appointments and the little girl inside my mind looked up at her Dad desperately
hoping he would say everything was ok.

He stared back with kind eyes, watching me grasp for the reins of a horse that was never mine to ride.

In that quiet moment over iced tea and lemonade on the back deck, I felt my heart sync with every adult child who has been in this chair asking these questions holding back a river of tears.

And suddenly, I was every single one of us in dark
closets sorting through drawers of jewelry, worn out
sneakers and treasured keepsakes, while clutching mom's
bathrobe wondering how long the smell of her perfume
will remain.

No matter how hard we try, we don't get to skip this part in
our human story.
Growing old together is a privilege not for the faint of heart.
Our most important job is to arrive at the beauty of
the moment before us.

Thank you is a prayer.

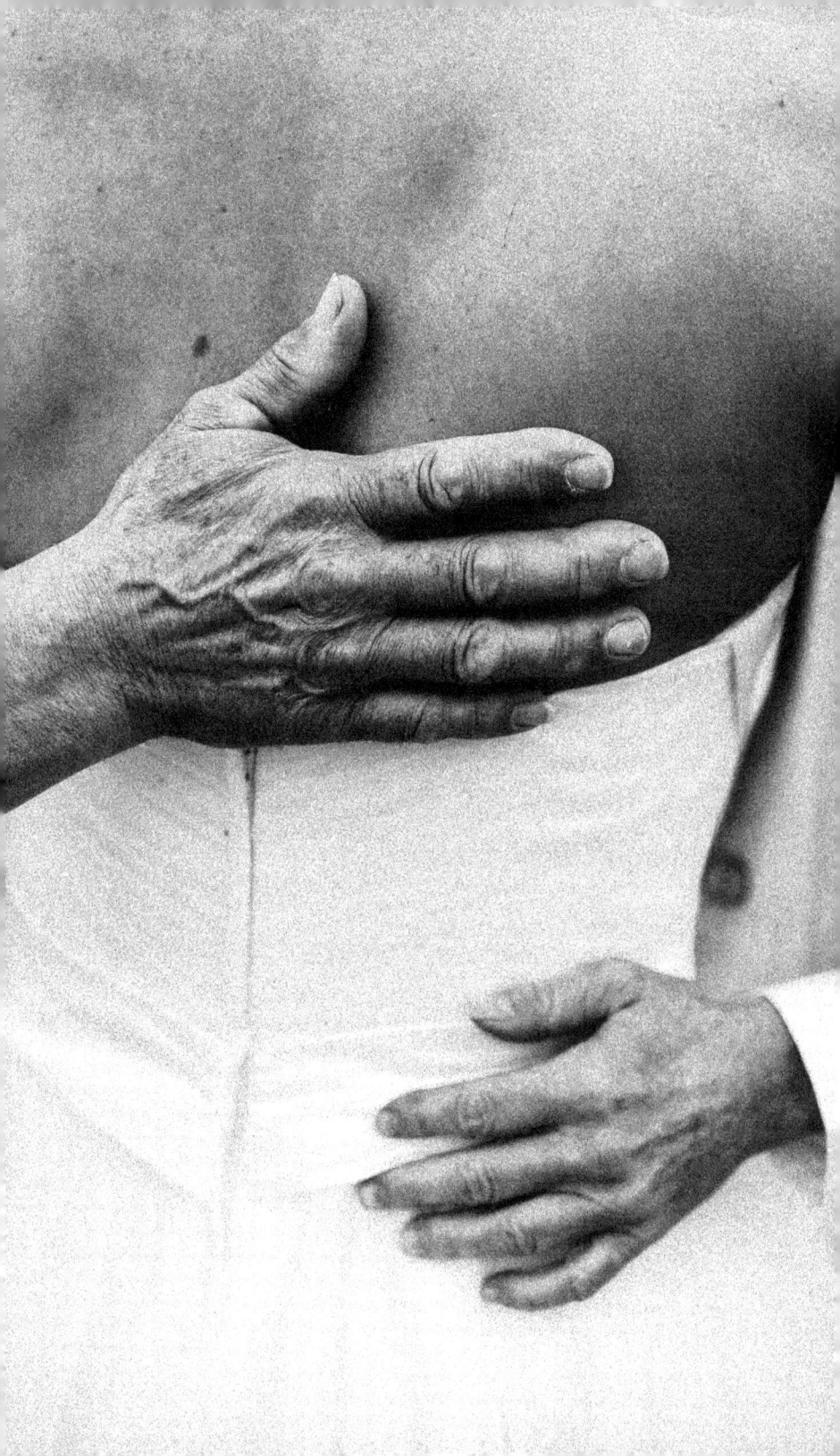

Mama Bird

She built a world of whimsy and wonder.
With tired wings and her whole heart, she nourished and
protected and gave every bit of herself to the dream of
our becoming.
When it was time, she took her baby birds to the edge of
the world and showed us how to fly.
We stretched our wings to soar over treetops and mountains
and far away lands.
Over miles and years, we grew into the birds we were
meant to be.
Never forgetting our way back home.

Let your he(art) be your guide.

Lemons

I'm sitting in my living room wearing my winter coat as I weep on the oversized chair in the corner.
My dog is sitting atop the couch staring at me as I wipe tears from my cheeks.

I'm reading my most beloved author's words on the page –
it's a story about a homeless man beating his chest and yelling across the street, tired of not being seen or heard.

I close the pages and turn the book over in my hands, more page corners folded than not, the underlined passages calling me back at a moment's notice.
I'm weeping in a chair reading these words, feeling more seen by this person I may never meet, than those I do daily life with.

I'm weeping in a chair and I have to get lemons.
My family will be home soon and the pizza crust I promised is still at the store.
I'm weeping over these words and the tomorrow me is begging for her lemons.

So I wipe my tears and go.
I shuffle through the store meeting the eyes of others who
undoubtedly have big feelings locked up inside like the ones
I am carrying tonight, too.
I do my best to be warm and kind with my eyes.
It's New England in the middle of winter.
The snowbanks are sandy and not good for much more than
reminding us that spring is still weeks away.

I thank the cashier and wheel my way through the parking lot.
I pull in the driveway just in time to greet my family as they
arrive home.
My daughter leaps out of the truck and runs to me.

Everything rejoins itself; the fog of my heavy feelings
evaporates into thin air, and in that moment, I realize
I forgot the lemons.

Unlocked

Tell me dear one, what words do you need to hear?
Which sentence will unlock you from these chains?
Which arrangement of syllables will swing open the door to the cage you entered all those years ago?
Tell me so I can speak them to you.
Tell me so I can be there for the moment you emerge.
Tell me so I can come with you.

We've become masters
at solving the world's most
complicated problems,

only to forget that
love was never supposed to be
a complicated problem.

The Ghost of Ambition

How much time do we spend trying to predict a future
that may never come?
How much of ourselves do we dedicate to plans and
pathways we may never pursue?
Which parts of us crave the certainty of what's next, while
daring to stay open to the whisper of the great unknown?

I threw out my planner this year and with it,
all of my best laid plans.
I revised my grand visions to meet only what's here and now.
There are moments I find myself expecting the ghost of
ambition to rise and revisit me.

I catch myself tracing over my lists and wracking my brain
as I await its arrival and the familiar press of its presence.
Yet, all I am met with is a soft silence, the beat of my own heart
and the gentle emergence of new words to arrange
until they fit.

Slow mornings and warm mugs make way for the world I've
always dreamt of, the one I am still learning to inhabit.

Remember to remember the magic of right now.

Belonging

Our innate need for belonging is often part of
how we give ourselves away.
We replace the power of pleasing with our
true nature of being pleased.
We seek what is outside in desperate attempt to
heal what feels broken on the inside.
The toggle switch gets tripped and there we are
building bridges for someone else's dreams
while ours slowly fade into the background.
The sweet nectar of belonging seeks to satisfy an
ancient craving we've been thirsting for.
To belong to another is the gift that tastes sweeter when
we know how to receive the gift of our own presence.

Never forget...

You are a miracle in motion.
A one in 400 trillion chance.
The love of a lifetime.
The dream of dreams.
The cherry on top.
The answered prayer.

You are an *unrepeatable gift*.

The Gazelle

Sometimes the world moves too fast and I find myself asking too much of me.
Away I go, in the heat of the moment, pressing forward and forgetting my faith in what I cannot see.
It's in moments like these when I feel myself floating above the surface, losing my footing here on earth, unable to find the traction required to exist in this worldly plane.

Yet, no matter how far I strive to find the keys to success or the right answers along the way, the greatest gift I can give to the world is my whole heart.

They say that the best leader is the calmest person in the room, yet my heart flutters inside my chest like a gazelle in the field awaiting her fate for being born in a world where there are lions.
It is the ferocity of our faith that will save us from becoming the feast.

Our true nature is our greatest superpower.
Our capacity for courage our new gear.
Our generosity of spirit and the ways we were born to care for one another our blessing.

Being who we really are requires no gimmick or scheme, rather a devotion to what stirs us awake and the boldness to put the car in drive.
It's in the simplicity of being that we are free.

The River

Enter the river of your sadness.
Let its holy waters hold you, lift you, take you through
memory, space and time.
As we travel, we become lighter – our grip on what once
was somehow opens, making way for new understanding.
And here we are floating on our backs, looking up at the clouds,
weaving our way downstream.
Sorrow has a way of showing us who we really are and
what awaits us in the depths.
Loss, in all of its darkness, has a way of bringing us back
to the surface where we meet the light.

Closer to Shore

The house is a different kind of quiet when you're gone.
The bed is cold, and half-empty.
There is no doubt your love has brought me home.
Sometimes I worry about things I can't change.
I pray that the parts of us that have drifted out to sea won't
be lost in the mist of our own becoming.
I like it better when you're here, breathing next to me.
And in the dark of night, when I wake up with a shiver,
you're there, turning softly in your sleep -
pulling me closer to shore.

The Opponent

A voice with no owner spoke through me, "Are you ready to put this down now?"
This same voice has whispered to me throughout my days, reminding me of the moments I cannot unknow and the memories that have woven themselves together in the stories I have lived.

Reflecting back on the dots of my life, from survivor to speaker and little girl lost to a mother meeting herself at every age of her daughter's childhood along the way, all of it makes sense now.

One night, I listened to my husband singing our girl to sleep through the walls of our home here on the pond and out of nowhere the voice returned, "Are you ready to put this down now?"

"This" was the weighted vest of self-loathing and sharp criticism I obediently wore throughout my days.
It was there in every moment like a bitter old friend who centered her life around keeping me in my place.

I had built a muscle to outwork her, to overcome and outlast the inner pain that made everything so much harder.
It turns out that the depth of courage I had relied upon existed, most of all, because I needed it in order to endure my own crushing blows.

Are you ready to put this down now?
And in a whisper as the gentle song of crickets filled
the night sky,
I said, "Yes."

The Author

Do not be ashamed of the projections and reflections
cast upon you.
You are not the author of the stories they choose
to write about you.
You author you.
You write the story of your one precious life.
Make it one to remember.

Sailing

Being who I am is not an act of rebellion, it's one of reclamation, reunion, and coming home to Truth.
As children we are told our dreams of being dancers and singers and writers and astronauts are cute and unreasonable.
Over time, we learn that our dreams are a death sentence in this world of practicality and permission seeking we've been born to covet.
So we choose what's "safe" and surrender the truth of who we are to deadlines and proving.
We step away from our dreams in order to "save" ourselves from the struggle and end up in a life of suffering hidden behind endless pressure and TPS reports.
Then one day, we wake up with the words to a song or the stars in our eyes and we remember.
Our once wild and illogical dreams engulf us in wonder and ignite something we hid away long ago.
We catch the wind and we're sailing through a timeless sea – flying over waves being pulled by the current of what we came here to discover.

We must let out our sails and wait for the wind to remind us of what we've always known.
We are not here by accident.
We are so much more than cogs in the wheel.
We have the capacity to build a home with our bare hands and tear it to the ground in a day's work.
We get to start anew and begin again in any moment of our choosing.
No part of you is obligated to be anyone other than who you are.
Suffering is the red alert that something needs to change.
How long we live with the alarm blaring in the background is up to us.
Our anguish is not a badge to be won, rather an invitation to evolve.

Board by board

A dream home is built board by board, nail by nail, just as an artist commits to her canvas one brush stroke at a time.
Our dreams live beneath the repetitions that prepare us for the conception of what has been calling to us.
Like the sculpture hiding in the stone, our masterpiece is never far.
Our deepest work is to stay present to the practice of revealing what awaits.

Contentment is a cure.

Calmness a religion.

Caring about how you feel – *the compass.*

Instructions on How to Live

Discover what's yours.
Worship what belongs.
Claim every bit of what makes you come alive.
Let everything else fall away.

Commit to your sacred relationship with you.
Gift yourself the space to listen for the whispers.
Walk in the direction of your gifts.
Linger in the spaciousness of wonder.

Adorn yourself in what feels like home.
Drink in what soothes you more fully than you've ever known.
Hold the cup of your dreams lovingly in your hands.
Allow each sip to be a prayer.

Reunion

"But what do you really want?" she asked.
I stared blankly back at her realizing I didn't know how to answer the question.

Who was I to want when I already had so much?
Who was I to decide when so much had already been decided for me?
What was I to do when the master plan fell to pieces in my hands?

Ever the dutiful one, I had been building the life I believed was my only choice, until I woke one morning, and my living felt like a prison I could not escape.

Obligation and expectation guided my days.

The me I had quietly become was entirely new and she was ready to throw in the towel on this race to nowhere.

So I went to the beach with my journal and watched the waves crash on the rocky shore.
I drew another path on the page.
I said the words that needed to be spoken and in an instant, everything changed.

And so it is...

Sometimes the reclamation and the reckoning is the only answer to the question we never wanted to ask.

And the day came when
what once felt brave
became the way of
her being.

Wake up Singing

It's Tuesday morning and I'm blinking myself awake.
Her sweet voice floats down the hallway like a butterfly with no care but to catch wind on its way to the flower.
I wonder when the last time was that I woke up singing.
Life and tasks and pressure and time seemed to tick away this sweet part of me.
Her voice grew louder, and I heard her tiny feet hit the floor and the door open to a new day.
In an instant, I remember, I'm alive.
My only real work here is to wake up singing.

Oh, what a joy it is to be yours...

Light & Living Water

Feel it all.
Let it wash over you like a waterfall.
Emerge like a rainbow in the mist,
holographic magic, appearing in thin air.
Light and living water bringing forth the miracle of
your infinite existence.

You are magnificence in physical form.
Revel in the brilliance of your being.

There is undeniable beauty in you.
The more you do what brings you joy,
The more your life will brim with bliss.

Every breath is a chance to begin again.

Every moment
brings us closer to
touching all of time.

Without the courage to strike the match, there would be no fire.

Enter

When I'm sprinting around in effort to extinguish the fire of my fears, the only remedy is to slow down enough to stop it from spreading beyond where it began.

I stop to take in the textures of my life like the years gone by now nestled in the metal of my lovingly worn wedding band or the grooves in the wooden floors of our beloved home.

No matter how hard we effort to pay attention, the trees, like our loved ones seem to grow without anyone noticing, until one day you find yourself looking up in astonishment.

Entering our lives means listening for the heartbeats,
while forgiving and forging onward as
our hearts heal in the soft pauses of our days.
Time is not the enemy.
Each moment that ticks by is a chance to revere what is here.

I am not here to prove myself.
I am here to be myself.

Reflections

What happens when I "be" myself and everyone leaves?
What happens when honoring what feels holy to me makes others uncomfortable and cruel?

I was being myself and I was violated
I was being myself and they rejected me.
I was being myself and he almost left.
I was being myself and she wouldn't stop.

What if being myself only makes things worse?
What if being myself isn't enough?
What if being myself is the actual problem?

The times I've tried on another way of being are innumerable, like that dress on the rack you just know won't fit, but your friend pumps you up to try it,
"What's the worst that could happen?" She asks.
The worst that could happen?

It zips.
And you turn to look at yourself in the mirror and hardly recognize the girl staring back at you.

So you buy it and add it to the collection of things that you know will never see the light of day.
And those tiny, uncomfortable things staring back at you from the depths of your closet taunt you, and remind you of the lie that you're not enough - even for a $29 piece of polyester. Suddenly, we believe the lie and build a world around it.

The cutting words of loved ones nestle in our hearts like a stone sinking to the bottom of the pond never to be moved again. Our relationships, our friendships, our careers, our diets, our reason for being metamorphosize to match the narrative that feels safe and acceptable.

And it's here that we begin to lose touch with the most authentic parts of ourselves: the whispers, the longings, the sound of our own beating heart.
Onward we march, writing and living out chapters that feel like fiction in our souls.

But what needs to change is not us, it's the stories we adopt as truth, with their gaping holes and cheap endings.

It's in the depth where we discover the fragments that had been scratched from the page without our knowing.

It's in the sacred process of connecting the dots that leads us to true liberation.
We matter because *we are here.*
Each breath we draw from the well of all breathing is the confirmation of this.
How we be and do is who we are.
And so our work is to crawl our way out to the edge of our own conditioning to see our world with new eyes, again and again, until the end of time.

We matter because we are here.

The Miracle of Our Unfolding

A diner I love announced that it is closing forever today. Memories flooded my mind as I traced my steps over the threshold of warm hellos and joyful goodbyes.
Coming hungry, leaving full.

In this wave of nostalgia, I am transported back in time to moments like my first kiss and the taste of Big Red gum on both of our lips or the rush of freedom that coursed through my veins the first time I drove my 5-speed fire engine red Saab down those backroads all by myself.

It's these indelible notes that bring us back.
I used to worry there was something wrong with me for feeling this much, until I realized that this is what happens when we're paying attention.

Oh, how I wish we could slow down to see the miracle of our own unfolding and go back in time to sit in that booth once more to sip from a plastic cup with ice water that will never taste like this again.

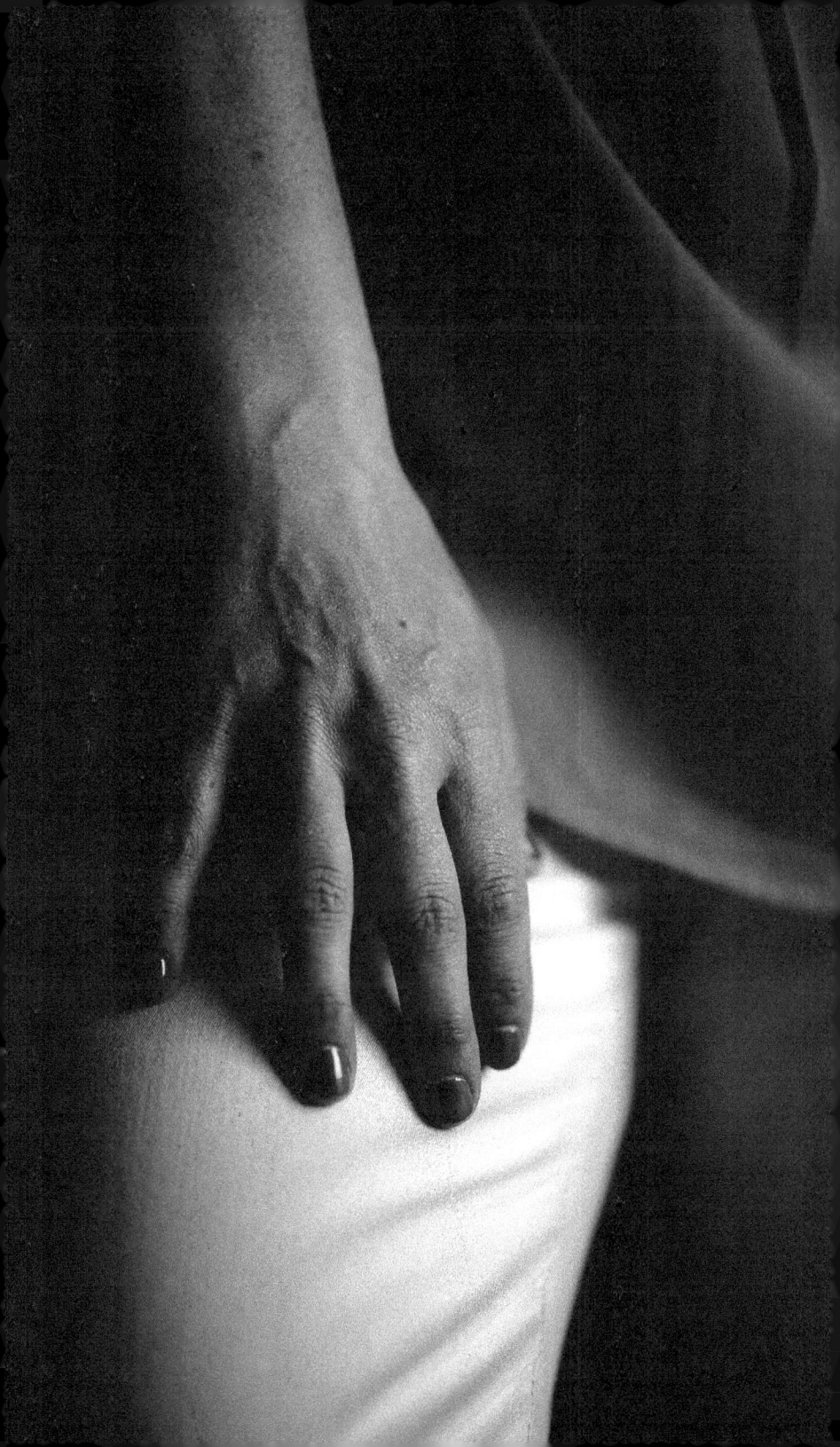

Birdsong

There's a bird outside my window singing a song
I've never heard before.
It's still mostly dark and it's taking me on a journey.
I didn't buy a ticket or know I would have a front row seat.
But I'm hanging on every note as I sip from my cup listening
to a symphony no one will ever hear, but me.

Turning Stones

There is no limit to the number of words I can string together, nor edge to how far my mind can go.
We're all here to fill the blank page of our being with what only we can define.

What do you believe?
What do you know?
What do you hold dear in ways that words cannot contain?
What makes your spirit soar – simply for the sake of soaring?
What makes you weep without warning?

Obligation eventually gives way to acceptance, like melting snow to the river.
And only what's essential remains, like love and light and the symphony of memories our lifetimes weave together while we're busying ourselves with becoming.

If we could only see what waits for us at the intersection of the infinite and our own blessed humanity, we would stop all of our seeking.

We would put down our plans and open our arms to the perfection of what's already here, while the birds chirp outside the window and the dog sighs at my feet.

Everything we need is before us.
Everything else is on the way.
I've come to discover that turning the stones of my past and opening the gift of my present is the only way to truly know this.

Becoming You

The more you, you become, the less they will matter.
But not at first.
At first your heart will break into a million pieces to see that they were always keeping score.
The perfect landing, the colossal misstep, every single gaffe tabulated on the page.
Until, blessedly, one day this rubric will mean nothing to you.
And in that moment, *you will be free.*

Do our problems still exist if we
stop believing in them?

Cease your suffering.
Surrender your pain.
Sync up with the stream of liberation.

Float.

Evolution

Stay nimble. Stay light.
Resist the urge to fight.
Exchange the revolution for the wonder of evolution.
Quantum wealth and next level health.
See it through. It starts with you.

Remember your future.
Catalyze your calling.
Dance with your desires.
Activate your ascension.

We

The softness I crave is mine to create.
The tenderness I long for starts with me.
Only, today, it feels hard, and I do too.
You're out in your ocean and I'm calling you home.
To me and to the we, we dreamt we could be.

Heartbreak

Each breath is a chance to begin again.
Each tiny expression of love and every thought that stretches a heart beyond its storied armor is a beginning.
May we give ourselves boundless grace and infinity chances at loving ourselves through the fog of our own disappointments.
May we have the courage to face our heartbreak in all its glory.
For the break cannot exist without the love.

What's Becoming

Fall is on the way.
I can see her in the golden glow illuminating branches.
I can hear her in the early morning whisper of summer leaving the pond.
I can feel her presence like I can the woman our sweet girl will one day grow into.
This art of feeling a future that's not yet here, like a world without my parents in it or a dog bed without our dear pup, roots me here.
It's a constant reminder to be where we are, to treasure our sacred now as these moments become memories.
Yet, the future has a way of pulling us away.
In a society that values progress over presence, the promise of achievement leads us down hallways we've been trained not to question.
Getting the degree because it's a requirement for the career our loved ones told us we should pursue or buying the house with the partner the world approves of are some of the ways we do this.
Consulting with a future that compels us into perpetual motion is a mode of hypervigilance that keeps the veil firmly in place.
Still, I can't help but feel a twinge of excitement as I watch the first leaf beginning to change.
The muse and her mystery of what's becoming is a rapture we cannot resist.

What's loftier than living well
in this one gorgeous life that
we've been given?

Chop Wood. Carry Water.

What if all of the things that feel so exponentially complicated are here only to remind us of how simple it can be?

Wake to greet the day.

Welcome in the light.

Nourish.

Chop wood.

Carry water.

Give thanks.

Rest.

Repeat.

Bones

What a wonder, this body that creaks and cracks,
and wilts with time.
It's the price of admission
and our sacred chance to be here.
Oh, how things change when I choose to
cherish these tired old bones.

Sister Pines

I went for a walk in the woods to find my way back home.
Too many days away makes for a distracted mind.
I placed my palm on the bark of an old tree hoping to seek
the wisdom of a being lifetimes older than me.
I breathed in the sweet scent of sister pines and ancient earth
remembering what can only be found in the forest.
This peace is an ever-present installation out here, if only it
were within me.

The Way Things End

Someone I love decided we were done.
There was no warning nor chance to reconcile or mend.
I woke up one morning and they were gone.
A collection of memories and old joys now sit enmeshed with a pile of unanswered questions.
The repeating loop of what and whys haunt me in the echo chamber of my mind.
I quieted my heart long enough to realize that sometimes the way things end is all we ever needed to know.
Sometimes the way things end is the blessing we didn't pray for.

For So Long

For so long, I thought something was wrong with me...
For wanting something different, for feeling another way,
for being the me I was born to be.
So I tried it all on – the lights and the hustle, the games and
the gossip.
I bought in and sold out, until I felt like I was melting and the
notion of masquerading as anyone but me felt like death.
There's a difference between authenticity and performing
for love.
Oh, how rare it is to meet what's real in a world that shames
and tames our tender hearts.

The Wild River of Her Heart

And one day she woke tired of holding back the wild river of her heart.
This deep surrender broke the dam she had built inside of herself all those years ago.
And she was free.

Love means devotion and devotion means love.

Devotion

He chose to stay.
Forever teaching me that
love means devotion and
devotion means love.
Enduring. Unending.
Together into forever.
Committing beyond vows and fear.
Giving into grace.
Handing over the armor of lifetimes before
so his tender heart could breathe again.

Bloom

Be tender with yourself.
You are a growing, breathing thing.
Like a flower springing from the earth – new and delicate,
yet strong enough to withstand the elements.
Allow yourself to take root.
Open to greet the softness of your being.
There is nothing to prove here.
Your singular kind of beauty is as original and rare as it gets.
Bloom from this knowing.

Technicolor Treasure

Stare into your own eyes.
See the Universe reflected in their sparkle.
You are a constellation of miracles and magic
unfolding in this exquisite moment.
The cosmic nature of your conception and the
stardust in your cells knows no bounds.
You are a technicolor treasure to behold.

Try softer. Let your hard edges fall away. repeated.

Why not love?

What if instead of fighting, we danced?
What if instead of criticizing, we embraced?
What if instead of condeming, we worshipped
the ground we walk upon?
There are infinite ways to respond...
Why not love?

The Language of My Soul

My mind endeavors to understand what only my heart can know.

Life is meant to be lived through the kaleidoscope of my senses, beyond the limited lens of my fearful brain.

No matter how hard I squint to see, I cannot comprehend what exists beyond words and reason.

It seems the language of my soul is a dialect I am still learning.

A tree doesn't fight the storm,
it trusts its roots.

These are the Days

I love waking up early in the dark hours before the world is with me.
There's a different kind of quiet here, and with it, a sense of clarity and space to see what the noise of the day often blurs.
I light a candle and grab a blanket and find my way back to me.

With soft eyes and a gentler heart, I wonder why it's so much easier to surrender here?

As I watch the candle flicker, I think of all the people I love – far and wide.
I wonder if they're awake and thinking thoughts no one will ever know about.
I wonder if they're writing love letters or sipping from their favorite mugs, too.

I center myself in the moment and remember that
these are the days.
The years tick by here and our bodies slowly wane.
We grow and grow until we become smaller in stature and more expansive in spirit.

My father's body is slowly changing.
He can't hear quite the same and sometimes I watch him sit
quietly as the chaos of family and grand babes swirl around and
I wonder where he is.
On a ski slope or a patch of open water in his mind?
Maybe he's back in Vietnam…

These moments remind me that now is the time…
To say what we need to say, to write the words, to show up
and tend to our sweet hearts, to love without holding back.

What matters is what matters.
These are the days.

Aborning Soul

The wild forest of your mind has held you hostage long enough.
Gather what you already know of yourself, like
sticks on the forest floor.

Bundle them up and carry them home.
Use them as kindling to warm yourself.

Ignite your soul from within.
Watch the shadows dance on the ceiling
as you breathe quietly in the solitude.

You are an aborning soul – ever-present,
ever-returning to your truest essence.
Hallelujah!

We can do extraordinary things.

Bend

There will be days when the light feels too bright.
There will be days when all that is good and wonderful in our world feels like a heavy weight.
When these clouds come, it is not our job to pretend ourselves away from what's before us.
Bending with the breeze until the shadows clear and going about our tending while we wait for the light to return is our only job.

Victory

The ultimate victory is putting our pain to work in the name of love.
Let your heartbreak give you hope.
Allow your pain to make way for possibility.
Alchemize your suffering into strength.
Rise from the ashes of your ache and soar.

Release All Pressure

Constriction pins us in.
Rigidity limits our choices.
There's nowhere to go inside the box.

For how long will we live with stiff necks and one-way tickets to the places we'd rather not go?

At some point, the only option is to open the valve.
Break free from the chains that bind.
Expand beyond the confines of where we've been to inhabit all of ourselves.

Sure, pressure makes diamonds, but we are more precious than any stone.

It's time for fluidity and flow,
For new arrangements and honest ways of expressing who we are.
Genius needs room to grow and blossom into being.

Release all pressure and live, dear one.

Forgiven

Forgive yourself for your transgressions.
Release yourself from the crushing weight of your regrets.
Unlock yourself from the chains you've worn for far too long.
Revel in how loved you know yourself to be.

*Does my body know of
the labels I've given it?
Or is it too busy doing what bodies do
and healing, instead?*

One

A baby comes forth from one egg.
It doesn't matter if you have access to infinity eggs -
to create life you only need one.
A soulmate, a beloved friend, a favorite author -
it's all about the one.

In our hurry to relieve ourselves of the fear of inertia or
insignificance, we lose sight of this simple truth.
We daunt ourselves with the challenge of being for everyone,
when that only carves us into caricatures of our truest selves,
leaving what's authentic to fall away for the sake of speed.

But a lasting reality is that no one is for everyone.
Our job is to remember that even the masses are made up of a
collection of ones.
What wonderful news.

You're not behind.
Start with one.

You are not behind.

Cease All Striving

Exhaustion reigns supreme in a world that values what's out more than what's in.
Fatigue fades us into the shadows of our truest selves.
The wisest parts of us are whispering, "
There has to be another way."

And then it arrives...
The wake up to shake up.
The emboldened invitation to *cease all striving*.

There is no departure needed when the yes belongs to you.
There is no overcompensation when we listen for the melody of our own soul.

Put on a song that brings you back.
Drop your phone in the drawer.
Unplug from the cycle of never-ending needs.

Swing open the doorway to your own golden center.
Rest your bones in the quiet for a while.
Take your time and breathe.

You have journeyed many miles to get here.

Efforting for what isn't is a form of self-torture.
To strive is to assume deficiency.
There is nothing lacking about you.

A rejuvenated you is the most glorious wellspring of possibility that exists.
Fill yourself to the brim.

Float

Put down your struggle.
Soak in your immeasurable depths.
Let go of what takes so you can convene with what contributes.

Immerse in the river of your being.
Release the tethers of your past.
Float in the stream of surrender and be free.

You are the gift you bring.

You are the gift you bring.

The Great Conjunction

History is happening.
The cosmos are conjoining.
Constellations are connecting.
Star seeds are stretching.
Souls are colliding.
Truth is being revealed.

We can no longer turn our gaze from the glimmer of galaxies
calling us to break free from the chains that have held us in fear.
We are so much more than we've been led to believe.
Boundless, beautiful beings dancing on a temporary planet
for a cause we'll never fully comprehend.
Dance on, dear one.

How can I love my life even more?
How can I ask for help even more?
How can I receive even more?
How can I relax even more?
How can I be me even more?

And the moment arrived when she
surrendered to the whisper of her soul
and the sweet call of her everlasting dreams.

say yes

Golden Possibility

Receive the blessing of what holds you, what surrounds you, what's already here.
Steady your deep need whispering from the valley of what's yet to be.
Commune with the splendor of what is.
You are golden possibility in flesh and bone.
You were a dream long before you took your first breath.
Your very existence is a priceless gift that will give on in perpetuity.
Anoint yourself with the crown of your capacity to love.
Walk in the majesty of your glorious existence.
There are no mistakes in the cosmic order.
You are the stuff of miracles and stardust perfectly made for this moment.

You are golden possibility. You are a priceless gift. You are the stuff of stardust. You are golden possibility. You are a priceless gift. You are the stuff of stardust. You are golden possibility. You are a priceless gift. You are the stuff of stardust. You are golden possibility. You are a priceless gift. You are the stuff of stardust. You are golden possibility. You are a priceless gift. You are the stuff of stardust. You are golden possibility. You are a priceless gift. You are the stuff of stardust. You are golden possibility. You are a priceless gift. You are the stuff of stardust. You are golden possibility. You are a priceless gift. You are the stuff of stardust. You are golden possibility. You are a priceless gift. You are the stuff of stardust. You are golden possibility. You are a priceless gift. You are the stuff of stardust. You are golden possibility. You are a priceless gift. You are the stuff of stardust. You are golden possibility. You are a priceless gift. You are the stuff of stardust. You are golden possibility. You are a priceless gift. You are the stuff of stardust. You are golden possibility. You are a priceless gift. You are the stuff of stardust. You are golden possibility. You are a priceless gift. You are the stuff of stardust. You are golden possibility. You are a priceless gift. You are the stuff of stardust. You are golden possibility. You are a priceless gift. You are the stuff of stardust. You are golden possibility.

If the dream is in you, it's for you.

ACKNOWLEDGEMENTS

To you, dear reader, you have journeyed from far and wide to here. I salute you. I honor you. I thank you for being the light and the constant companion in the hallways of my mind as I put these words on the page.

To my beloved students for your courage and resiliency. It is a profound privilege to know you, to walk with you and to witness your gorgeous expansion. You are a treasure, and your dreams are what make the world go round. Keep going.

To my dear friends and life-givers, Karin Haysbert, Cathy Heller, Julie Solomon, Jeanine Staples, Heidi Stevens, Heather Chauvin, Lisa Fraley, Carrie Montgomery, Laura Thompson Brady, Christina Neuner, Mia Whalley, Myrna Daramy, Kate Northrup, Allyson Byrd, Susie Moore, Deena Kretzer, Connelly Steward, Amber Frye, and Laurel Holland – thank you for championing my work and walking with me on this sacred path. What a gift your friendship is to me.

To my beloved sisters, Rachel Camfield, Liza Witonis, Jamie Clampet + Kristin Hubbard, for being the lighthouse in the storm of living, for the laughter, the text messages, the excitement at the smallest details, the check-ins, the encouragement and the endless inspiration in the ways you share your genius. You are my muses. I love each of you dearly.

Thank you Karen and KMD Books for helping bring this lifelong dream to fruition and to Cass for your art and brilliance in bringing this design to life. Dream team!

To my incredible photographer and dear friend, Lauren Bodwell. You are a treasure. Your art has brought life to my work in ways words cannot capture. You see what no one else can. I love and appreciate who you are. Thank you for sharing your heart so generously with me.

To Mark Nepo, your work has given me wings and changed me from the inside out. Thank you for your unwavering devotion to bring forth what you have discovered along the stream. It is a true joy to call you a friend.

To Adrea Peters, your steady guidance and love have been the soft place to land as I found my way home to this sacred work. Thank you for helping me find the courage to step into my writerly life and for leading the way with your own brilliance. I love you beyond words.

To the mentors that believed in me before I did, Mama Jean Mitchell, Rosemary Bredeson, Donna Thatcher, Dr. Hardy, Dot, Marty, Steve, Coach Jackson, Coach Mac, Mr. Veitenheimer, Professor Briand and Coach Pardo. Thank you.

To my dear family, Mom, Dad, Jake, Dee, Amy, Sheena + beloved ones, for being the steady in the waves of life. The world is a better place with each of you in it. Thank you for sharing your hearts with me and gifting me grace infinity times over. You are the truest definition of goodness there is. What a gift to get to be a part of this beautiful legacy of souls. I love you so.

To Ben + Anni, you are my dream of dreams, my inspiration and my North Star. I love you endlessly into lifetimes and beyond. Lucky me to get to be yours.

ABOUT AMBER

Amber Lilyestrom is a transformational business coach, branding expert, author and speaker.

Her work has been featured by Forbes, Entrepreneur and Working Mother Magazine and she has appeared on countless top-rated podcasts. Before launching her own company in 2014, she was one of the nation's top sports marketing professionals and taught at the University of New Hampshire.

Today, Amber helps visionary entrepreneurs and CEOs align their purpose with their sacred work in the world. Her genius is in helping them position themselves for deeper connection to their calling through her life-changing Brand Love Method™.

Amber lives with her husband, Ben, and daughter, Annika, on the pond in the woods of New Hampshire. When she's not writing, she's out in her kayak or wandering through the forest with her beloved husky pup Nika.

Connect with Amber on Instagram @amberlilyestrom or over at amberlilyestrom.com

OTHER TITLES
by Amber Lilyestrom

Grab a copy at amberlilyestrom.com

www.ingramcontent.com/pod-product-compliance
Lightning Source LLC
Chambersburg PA
CBHW062026290426
44108CB00025B/2800